EVERYONE EATS™

POULTRY

Jillian Powell

RSVP

**RAINTREE
STECK-VAUGHN**
P U B L I S H E R S
The Steck-Vaughn Company

Austin, Texas

Titles in the Series

BREAD EGGS FISH FRUIT
MILK PASTA POTATOES
POULTRY RICE VEGETABLES

Published by Raintree Steck-Vaughn Publishers, an imprint of Steck-Vaughn Company
Everyone Eats™ is a trademark of Steck-Vaughn Company

Library of Congress Cataloging-in-Publication Data
Powell, Jillian.
Poultry / Jillian Powell.
p.   cm.—(Everyone eats)
Includes bibliographical references and index.
ISBN 0-8172-4767-X
1. Cookery (Poultry)—Juvenile literature.
2. Poultry—Juvenile literature.
I. Title. II. Series: Powell, Jillian. Everyone eats.
TX750.P69   1997
641.6'65—dc21   96-29686

Printed in Italy. Bound in the United States.
1 2 3 4 5 6 7 8 9 0 01 00 99 98 97

Picture acknowledgments

Cephas 4 (top), 8 (top), 11, 13 (bottom), 16 (top), 17 (bottom), 19 (bottom), 20, 21 (both), 22 (top), 23, 25; Chapel Studios 6, 10 (bottom), 18, 19 (top), 22 (bottom); James Davis Travel Photography 8 (bottom), 24 (top); Mary Evans 7 (both), 9, 24 (bottom); Eye Ubiquitous contents page, 5, 10 (top), 13 (top), 14 (both); Life File 12, 15, 16 (bottom), 17 (top); Wayland Picture Library title page, 4 (bottom)

Contents

What Is Poultry?

Poultry is the word we use for birds that are raised for their meat, like chickens, turkeys, ducks, geese, and guinea fowl. Wild birds that people hunt for their meat, such as grouse and pheasants, are called game. People have raised poultry for thousands of years. It is eaten all over the world by people of many different cultures and religions.

▲ Poultry that has been prepared for cooking. From left to right, they are chicken, poussin (a small, young chicken), and guinea fowl.

▶ Chicken is a popular food all over the world. Today, we eat ten times the number of chickens than were eaten fifty years ago.

Poultry has always been a popular food for feasts and celebrations. For many centuries, chickens, turkeys, and geese were expensive, and they were fattened for feasts on special occasions. With modern farming methods, in many parts of the world poultry is produced much more cheaply and is now eaten year-round for everyday meals. Most poultry today is farmed on big factory farms.

Poultry can be an important part of a balanced diet. Chicken and turkey are the most widely eaten poultry. The meat contains lots of protein, vitamins, and minerals but is low in fat, which makes it a healthful food. Chicken is used for many dishes, from Spanish paella and Chinese chow mein, to roasts and stir-frys. It is also a popular fast food, in the form of chicken wings, nuggets, drumsticks, and even burgers.

▼ Ducks foraging for food in a farmyard. All over the world, many people still keep poultry in backyards, as they have done for thousands of years.

Poultry Long Ago

Medieval feasts sometimes included strange dishes. Cokagrys was made by cutting a chicken and a pig in half and sewing them together.

◀ All chickens, like this cockerel from Sri Lanka, are ancestors of the wild forest birds that lived thousands of years ago.

Early peoples trapped wild birds, including ducks and geese, and roasted them over open fires. They may also have dried the meat in the wind or in wood smoke to store it through the winter months. By about 4000 B.C., people had learned how to tame and keep the red jungle fowl that lived wild in the forests of India and southeast Asia. Gradually, these birds spread to different parts of the world.

The ancient Chinese, Egyptians, Greeks, and Romans raised chickens, ducks, and geese. The Romans served cooked poultry with spicy sauces. Aside from their use as food, chickens also served as religious sacrifices. And cockfighting was a popular entertainment.

This Egyptian wall painting from 1500 B.C. shows wild birds being hunted for their meat.

A "chicken man" from 1647

Medieval poulterers sold both domestic and wild birds caught by fowlers using nets and traps, and stores in London sold roasted birds. In the country, most people kept a few hens and sometimes geese and ducks. Hens that were too old to lay eggs were boiled in a pot.

For special occasions and feasts, poultry was fattened up and baked in pastry cases or roasted with rich fruit stuffing and spicy sauces. Cooks used saffron or gold leaf to make a roast look golden, and for the most important feasts, they stuffed several birds one inside another.

Poultry in the Past

Turkeys first lived wild in Central and North America, where Native Americans used their feathers to decorate headdresses. In the sixteenth century, the Spanish conquistadors brought back turkeys to Europe, where they became known as "Indian chicken." Until that time, roast swan and peacock had been the traditional feast dishes of the rich. During the seventeenth and eighteenth centuries, flocks of turkeys were marched to market in London on foot, wearing leather boots or tar on their feet to protect them.

▲ A Thanksgiving meal of roast turkey. The turkey is traditionally served with gravy and cranberry sauce.

During the seventeenth century, cooks stored poultry by cooking it and then potting it in butter or pickling it in wine or vinegar. Poultry was also boiled in a pot, baked in pastry, or roasted with fruit and spices. One of the most impressive feast dishes was Yorkshire Christmas pie, made by baking layers of turkey, goose, chicken, partridge, and pigeon with butter in pastry.

Wild turkeys were caught and roasted for the first Thanksgiving feast, held by the Pilgrims in 1621. Turkey is still the central part of the Thanksgiving meal in the United States today.

▶ Guinea fowl originally came from Africa, and wild guinea fowl like these can still be found there.

By Victorian times (1837–1901), roast goose had become the favorite Christmas dish in Great Britain and other European countries.

Most poultry was kept free-range until the 1940s. During World War II (1939–1945), many people in Europe kept hens in their backyards while there was a shortage of fresh eggs and meat in the stores. After the war, farmers began breeding some chickens especially for their meat. They kept chickens and other poultry in large barns or in battery cages on egg farms.

▲ A Victorian family choosing their Christmas goose

Guinea fowl were once called "turkeys" because they first came to Europe through Turkey. Later, wild birds found in North America were also called turkeys because they looked similar to guinea fowl.

The Food in Poultry

Poultry meat is a good source of protein. A 4-ounce serving of chicken or turkey provides about half the protein an average person needs every day. The protein in poultry is easy to digest, so it is especially good for people who are sick or elderly.

A healthy diet is low in fat, especially saturated fats, which are found mainly in meat and dairy foods. Poultry is a healthful food because it is lower in fat than many foods, including most other kinds of meat. Eating less fat helps reduce the cholesterol in our blood. Too much cholesterol can lead to heart disease. A low-fat diet can also help protect us against other serious diseases.

▲ Boneless, skinless chicken breasts. The fat content of poultry is reduced if the skin is removed before cooking, because most of the fat is found just under the skin.

▶ Poultry is a nutritious, low-fat food that contains lots of protein. Protein helps us grow and repair our bodies to stay healthy and active.

Duck and goose contain more fat than chicken and turkey, but all poultry contains polyunsaturated fatty acids, which can help reduce cholesterol.

Poultry contains vitamins B and C and minerals like iron and zinc, which we need to keep us healthy. Poultry meat can be cooked and served with other healthful foods, such as salads, fresh vegetables, and fruit, as part of a balanced diet.

◀ Stir-frying is a healthful, low-fat method of cooking poultry. Broiling and steaming are also low-fat, healthful cooking methods.

4 oz. of chicken breast (meat only) provides:
25. 6 g protein
1.6 g fat
124 calories

4 oz. of duck provides:
20. 8 g protein
6.8 g fat
148 calories

Chicken Farming

Farmers raise poultry for meat or eggs. Chickens farmed for meat are called broilers or roasters. They have been bred to fatten quickly.

Chicks hatch from eggs in incubators that are kept at the temperature of a hen's body. When they are one day old, they are moved to poultry farms. At first, they live in brooders, which are sheds kept warm by infrared lamps.

Then, the farmer moves the chicks into deep-litter barns, which are large sheds with straw or wood shavings on the floor to collect their droppings. Up to 20,000 birds can live together in a barn. The barn must be kept clean and airy and have perches where the chickens can roost at night.

▶ Young chicks being fed at a chicken farm in Venezuela. Chicks are fed on special chick feed, which contains protein to help them grow fast.

12

Farming chickens in this way produces cheap meat, but the chickens have very little freedom.

Chickens are given water and food that contains cereals and vegetable and animal protein as well as grit to help them digest it. The food may also contain extra vitamins and minerals and antibiotics to prevent disease.

Chickens are killed when they are about 42 days old. Poussins, which are small, young chickens, are killed when they are only 28 days old. The birds are loaded into crates and taken by truck to a meat-processing plant, where they are killed. They are hung by their feet from moving belts and given an electric shock to stun them before their throats are cut by machine blades. The birds are then plucked by machines, ready for preparation and packing, for delivery to stores and supermarkets.

Most chickens are processed by machines, but on many farms around the world, plucking is still carried out by hand.

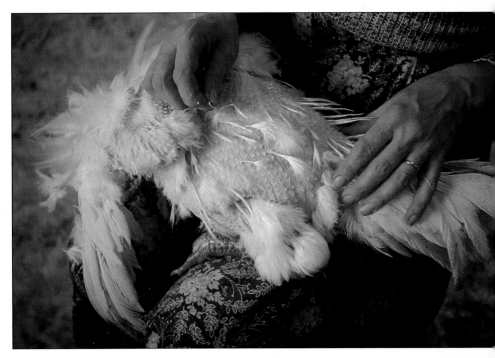

Poultry Farming

Turkeys and guinea fowl can be farmed in deep-litter barns. Turkey eggs are hatched in incubators. As one-day-old poults, they are moved to brooders, where they are kept warm for a few weeks. Then they are kept in barns with the sides open to the air and straw or wood shavings on the floor. One shed can house up to 10,000 birds.

The birds are given water and food that contains protein to help them grow fast, and antibiotics to prevent disease. Turkeys are killed when they are between 12 and 26 weeks old.

Guinea fowl are farmed in deep-litter barns and killed when they are nine or ten weeks old. Ducks are kept in barns or yards and are killed at seven or eight weeks, when they weigh 3–6 pounds.

▲ This duck farm is in a dry, desert area in Egypt. Water was taken from the Nile River to fill the pond.

▶ Turkeys on a large poultry farm in Greece

Many people think that factory farming is cruel. Some farmers raise poultry using a free-range system. Most free-range poultry live in sheds but spend about half their lives in outdoor runs, where they can scratch around for food. The farmer gives them fresh water and extra food containing protein. This is a more expensive way to produce poultry, but the birds live a more natural life.

Organic farmers raise poultry in free-range conditions without using chemicals. Organic farming is thought to be better for the environment.

▲ Free-range geese grazing in a frosty field in winter

Processing Poultry

Poultry is sold fresh or frozen or is processed to make soup or prepared dishes that are chilled or frozen.

At the meat-processing plant, factory workers remove the heads, feet, and offal. For freezing, poultry is first chilled in water to stop bacteria from growing. Then it is dried, weighed, and packed before it is frozen in huge blast freezers. "Oven ready" poultry may be stuffed and have fats and flavorings added under the skin.

Poultry portions can be coated with flaked potato, bread crumbs, or batter and sold chilled or frozen. Meat stripped from the bones is chopped up and mixed with soy protein, then shaped into sticks, rolls, sausages, nuggets, or burgers.

▲ Fresh poultry, like this chicken, is chilled and packed whole or cut into portions such as breasts, thighs, drumsticks, and wings.

◀ Chicken or turkey nuggets like these are coated in batter or bread crumbs and sold as prepared meals or fast food.

Poultry meat can be used to make soups, sandwich spreads, and pot pies. Prepared meals include poultry that has been cooked in sauces then canned, chilled, or frozen, ready to reheat in an oven or microwave. Poultry is also used for fast foods, such as deep-fried chicken wings and nuggets.

Chickens' and ducks' feet may be sent to the Far East, where they are eaten as a delicacy. Poultry offal that humans do not eat is cooked at very high temperatures to kill all bacteria then used in animal feed and fertilizers.

▲ This man in Cambodia is selling feather dusters made of dyed poultry feathers. Feathers are also used to stuff pillows, cushions, and comforters.

Poultry livers may be sold separately or made into liver paté. Foie gras is a very rich paté from France, made with the livers of geese or ducks. The birds are force-fed with corn to fatten them and to enlarge their livers.

► This uncooked goose liver will be used to make foie gras paté.

Cooking Poultry

There are many ways to cook poultry. It can be roasted, boiled, stewed, broiled, grilled, fried, stir-fried, barbecued, steamed, or microwaved.

Whole birds are usually roasted. Portions such as the breast are good for broiling, barbecuing, steaming, or stir-frying to preserve flavor and moisture. Thighs and drumsticks are good for longer methods of cooking such as stewing and in casseroles. Chopped or ground poultry meat can be used to make burgers, meat sauces, and pot pies.

Low-fat methods such as grilling, steaming, and stir-frying are the healthiest ways to cook poultry.

▲ A whole roasted chicken. The best way to test if a roasted bird is thoroughly cooked is to pierce the fattest part of the leg. When it is properly cooked, the juices run clear, not pink or red.

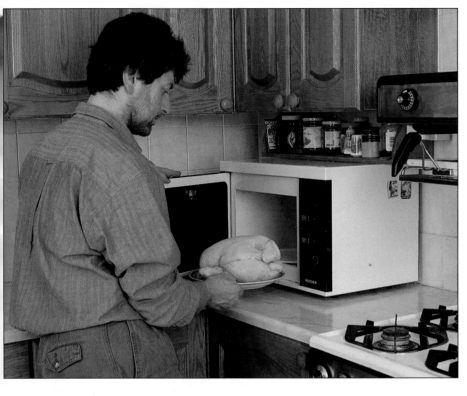

Poultry must be cooked thoroughly, because it can contain the bacteria salmonella and campylobacter, which can cause food poisoning. Microwaving is a good way of ensuring that poultry is cooked through.

Fresh poultry should be kept in a refrigerator at below 40°F and eaten within two to three days. It is important to keep raw poultry away from cooked foods.

Frozen poultry must be thoroughly defrosted before cooking. It should be defrosted in a refrigerator. A whole chicken will take at least 24 hours, and a larger turkey or goose may need more than three days to defrost.

A duck steaming in a bamboo basket over boiling water. This is a healthful way of cooking and is popular in the Far East.

Poultry Dishes from Around the World

Poultry is eaten all over the world by people of many different cultures and religions.

Chicken chow mein is a Chinese dish of chicken, stir-fried with ham, mushrooms, bamboo shoots, and Chinese cabbage, flavored with rice wine and soy sauce and served with fried noodles.

▲ The French dish coq au vin (chicken in wine) is popular in many countries. It is a casserole of chicken, bacon, onions, mushrooms, and herbs in red wine.

The Russian dish of chicken Kiev is made by folding pieces of chicken around a filling of butter, garlic, and parsley, then coating them with bread crumbs and deep-frying them.

Paella is a Spanish rice dish made with chicken, shellfish and vegetables, cooked in a large pan called a paellera.

20

Chicken kishk is an Egyptian dish made with pieces of chicken served with rice and a yogurt sauce thickened with kishk (a kind of dried cracked wheat).

Indonesian satay consists of pieces of chicken grilled on bamboo sticks and served with a peanut-flavored dipping sauce. Jerked chicken is a Caribbean dish using a mix of hot spices.

Chicken is often used to make soup. Waterzooi is a Belgian soup made by cooking chicken in white wine and stock, then thickening it with egg yolks and cream. Mulligatawny is a hot and spicy chicken soup from India, containing chilies and spices. Cock-a-leekie is a Scottish soup made of chicken boiled with pearl barley, leeks, and prunes.

▲ In Africa and the Caribbean, hot spices are added to chicken to make this dish, called jambalaya.

◀ In Great Britain and other parts of Europe, it is traditional to roast a turkey or goose for Christmas. A Christmas goose like this is often served with roasted potatoes and vegetables.

Poultry Cooking Around the World

In many parts of the world, poultry is roasted for special occasions. The Chinese eat chicken to celebrate birthdays, weddings, and holidays.

Cooks chop the roasted poultry into pieces, then serve it on a large plate. Most people prefer the dark meat eaten from bones like thighs and drumsticks. The white meat is served to children.

▲ Japanese Yakitori bars like this sell mainly chicken snacks, like kebabs of meat, livers, hearts, wings, and skin, which are dipped in soy sauce.

▼ Tandoori chicken, an Indian dish of chicken marinated in yogurt, chilies, and spices and traditionally cooked in a clay tandoor oven

Every part of the bird, including the heart, liver, and feet, is used in special dishes.

Duck is smoked or air-dried then roasted to make the skin really crisp.

Two duck dishes from Thailand—slices of roast duck served with sauce and a duck curry.

In African, Caribbean, Indian, and Far Eastern cooking, poultry is often marinated in spices before cooking, to add color and flavor.

In the Middle East, the meat from young poultry is often grilled. Older birds are stuffed, then roasted or steamed, or stewed with vegetables, dried fruit, herbs, and spices.

In North Africa, chicken is often cooked in a tagine, which is a clay pot with a cone-shaped lid. Dried fruit, almonds, lemons, and olives may be added for flavor.

The Aztecs, who lived in Central America until the sixteenth century, raised turkeys. They invented the dish mole poblano de guajolote, which is made with turkey cooked in a sauce containing chili peppers, nuts, and chocolate. The dish is still cooked and is traditionally served at feasts and celebrations.

Customs and Beliefs

▲ On Christian church spires, weather vanes like this are shaped like cockerels as a symbol of protection against evil.

Cockerels, young male fowls, feature in folklore all over the world. Cockfighting has linked them with bravery and fighting. They have also been seen as representing new life, because they crow at dawn. In classical myth, the cockerel was sacred to the god Apollo.

Cockerels are often seen as messengers, warning of danger or death. They have also been associated with magic and witchcraft, and people once believed that cockerels could scare away ghosts.

▶ This picture shows Romans carrying some geese in a procession. In 390 B.C., the noisy geese had warned the Romans that they were about to be attacked by the Gauls. The Romans carried a golden goose in procession to the Capitoline Hill every year to celebrate the event.

The "cock of Barcelos" is a Portuguese story about a cockerel that was roasted and served to a judge who had just sentenced a pilgrim to be hanged. The cockerel came back to life and told the judge that the pilgrim was innocent. The judge gave the pilgrim his freedom. A similar story is told in parts of Spain, and in one town a live cockerel is kept in the church.

In Japan, cockerels wander freely in temples and are not to be harmed or killed. In China, white cockerels are believed to protect against evil spirits. The cockerel is also important in Islamic belief because it was the bird seen in the first heaven by Muhammad.

In Africa, parts of Asia, and the Pacific countries, cockerels are seen as messengers from beyond our world. Some tribal peoples still kill cockerels as religious sacrifices and believe that they can tell the future by examining the dead birds' internal parts.

Geese appear in nursery rhymes and folk tales, such as "The goose that laid the golden egg." This story is about a Greek man who has a goose that lays golden eggs. The greedy man kills the goose so he can take all her golden eggs and so loses his magic supply of gold.

◀ A model of the Cock of Barcelos. Painted cockerels like this can be seen all over Portugal.

Poultry Recipes for You to Try

Lemon Chicken

To serve four people, you will need:

4 skinless, boneless chicken breast
  halves
7 tablespoons butter, softened
juice of 1 lemon

grated zest of 1 lemon
$\frac{1}{3}$ cup of sour cream
pinch of salt and pepper
1 tablespoon water

1 Ask an adult to help you to heat the oven to 375°F. Put the butter and the lemon zest into a bowl and mix together well.

2 Ask an adult to help you to make three diagonal cuts in each chicken breast, then rub the butter into the cuts.

3 Arrange the chicken pieces in a shallow ovenproof dish. Sprinkle with the lemon juice, salt and pepper. Cook in the oven for about 25 minutes, until the chicken is cooked through. Lift the chicken into another dish and keep it warm.

4 Add the water to the cooking dish, and stir it around, scraping up any juices. Warm in the oven or on the top of the stove for one or two minutes, then stir in the sour cream, and heat through for another few minutes. (Do not boil.) When it is hot, pour the sauce over the chicken.

Serve with fresh vegetables or a salad.

Turkey Bolognaise

To serve four people, you will need:

1 lb. raw turkey, ground
1 medium onion, chopped
l green pepper, chopped
1 14 oz. can tomatoes, chopped
1 garlic clove, crushed
1 tablespoon tomato paste

1 teaspoon chopped herbs
2 tablespoons olive oil
$\frac{1}{3}$ cup chicken, turkey, or
  vegetable stock
pinch of salt and pepper
$\frac{2}{3}$ lb. dried spaghetti

1 Ask an adult to help you heat the oil in a pan until hot. Add the garlic and the ground turkey. Stirring all the time, cook until the meat is no longer pink.

2 Add the rest of the ingredients, except for the spaghetti, and stir well. Cover the pan so it is just bubbling and cook for about 15–20 minutes.

3 While the turkey sauce is cooking, ask an adult to help you bring 3 qts. of water to a boil in a large pot.

4 Add the spaghetti and a pinch of salt. Stir, and bring the water back to the boil, then cover and cook for as long as it tells you on the spaghetti package (usually about 9–11 minutes).

5 When the spaghetti is cooked, ask an adult to help you drain it in a colander. Put it into a warmed dish and pour the turkey sauce on top.

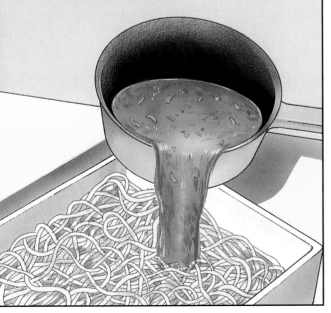

Serve with a salad.

Glossary

antibiotics Medicines used to destroy bacteria and cure some illnesses.

bacteria Tiny living things that have only one cell. Some are helpful but others can be harmful.

battery cages Cages in sheds used for keeping chickens, usually for their eggs.

bazaars Markets.

blast freezer Freezer that freezes food with blasts of cold air.

calories A measurement of the energy in food.

cholesterol A substance found in our bodies and some foods. Too much cholesterol can cause heart disease.

classical myth Traditional stories from ancient Greece or Rome.

conquistadors Spanish explorers who conquered Mexico and parts of South America in the fifteenth and sixteenth centuries.

defrosted Thawed out, so that no ice is left.

delicacy Food that is eaten as a special treat.

factory farms Farms where food is produced as quickly and cheaply as possible.

food poisoning An illness caused by eating food that contains certain types of bacteria.

folklore Stories, myths, and legends of certain peoples or areas.

fowlers Wild bird catchers.

free-range farming A system of keeping farm animals or poultry that allows them to spend some of their lives outdoors.

incubators Machines that keep eggs warm, ready for hatching.

infrared Describing certain light rays that cannot be seen but produce heat.

kebabs Grilled meat or vegetables, usually threaded onto sticks and sometimes marinated before being cooked.

marinated Soaked in a liquid before cooking. The liquid may contain vinegar, oil, herbs, or spices.

medieval From the period of the sixth to the fifteenth century.

minerals Substances found in some foods, which we need to keep us healthy.

nutrient Anything in food that is needed for health, such as vitamins, protein, minerals, etc.

nutritious Having food value.

offal Heart, liver, and other body organs.

organic farming A system of farming without using chemicals.

plucked With feathers removed.

30

polyunsaturated fatty acid A kind of fat found in some foods, which can lower cholesterol in the blood.

poulterers People who own or work in stores selling poultry.

poults Young turkeys or pheasants.

predators Animals or birds that eat other animals or birds.

processed Prepared for storage or cooking.

sacrifice Something offered up or given up for religious or other reasons.

saffron The orange part of a crocus flower, which is used for coloring and flavoring food.

saturated fat A kind of fat found in some foods. Too much saturated fat can cause heart disease.

spires Tall pointed towers on top of churches or other buildings.

stir-frying A way of cooking food quickly by stirring it in a small amount of hot oil in a wok (Chinese frying pan) or a frying pan.

tribal Of peoples who live in tribes, or groups, under a leader and share history and beliefs.

Victorians People living in England during the reign of Queen Victoria (1837–1901).

vitamins Substances found in some foods. We need vitamins to keep us healthy.

weather vanes Objects that are marked with the points of the compass and spin in the wind to show wind direction.

Books to Read

Chicken Cookbook. Westport, CT: Joshua Morris Publishing, Inc. 1995.

Cooper, Jason. *Turkeys*. Barnyard Friends. Vero Beach, FL: Rourke Book Co., 1995.

Potter, Tessa. *Ducks & Geese*. Animal World. Austin, TX: Raintree Steck-Vaughn, 1990.

Pulleyn, Micah & Bracken, Sarah. *Kids in the Kitchen: Delicious, Fun, & Healthy Recipes to Cook and Bake*. New York: Sterling Publishing, Inc., 1995.

Willan, Anne. *Chicken Classics*. Anne Willan's Look and Cook. New York: Dorling Kindersley, 1992.

Index

Numbers in **bold** show subjects that appear in pictures.